207th Bone

207th Bone

written by Zhou Li

translated by Xi Nan

The 207th Bone

Copyright © 2020 by Zhou Li

Translation copyright © 2020 by Xi Nan

All Rights Reserved. No part of this book may be reproduced in any form, or by any electronic or mechanical means, without the explicit consent of the publisher, except in the case of excerpts, critical reviews, or articles.

Printed in the United States of America

FIRST ENGLISH-LANGUAGE EDITION

ISBN 978-1-7341142-4-9

Simi Press
www.simipress.com
simieditions@gmail.com

Everyone who comes to this world comes with desires. We eat, sleep, fall in love... These are all natural impulses. And what is poetry? I think it is also a kind of desire. In their subconsciousness, every individual desires to be understood and recognized by others. This is probably where my poems were born.

Zhou Li

Translator's Introduction

In this poetry collection written by the Chinese poet Zhou Li (周立), the poems have no title and are only separated by blank lines. This doesn't seem to be the author's deliberate arrangement; he just let the poems be what they are. Much like a person's daily life: every day, week, month or year that passes does not have a definite theme, but this does not hinder every day from becoming every day and every year becoming every year. The days we spend may be happy, depressing, painful, empty, or even despairing. So are these poems; their existence is their meaning. They are not higher or lower than life itself.

It is a personal book, like a spiritual conversation with oneself, or short records of life and emotional fragments in the passage of time; it is some secret part of a person, suitable for reading when one feels sad, or on rainy days, nights, or when suffering from insomnia, and so forth—you will easily find resonation. You will see a man's desires, love, confusion, puzzles in life, and even politics. The poems are sorrowful and despairing; fortunately, they are also very light. You can pick the book up at any time, open any page to start reading, and then put it down any time. Perhaps it can also be said that these poems are our "unbearable lightness of being."

Although from different countries, time zones, geographical and political environments, readers will see their own traces and shadows in these poems—your desires, life, the puzzles you are facing—are all mirrored at another place on earth, on another person who is similar to you but also completely different. Zhou Li is experiencing exactly the same things many people on Earth are experiencing.

Zhou Li is a poet, of course. In addition, he is a doctor at a hospital, raises more than one hundred tortoises at home, is an insomniac, a middle-aged man who often regrets and hesitates... And sometimes he's just one of many faces in the crowd, just like you and me. He lives in a small town with hills behind it and the sea in the front in southeastern China. According to him, it is a magical place, a blessed land, and the frequent surrounding storms seldom affect his town.

Zhou Li has used simple and concise oral language to write these poems; it is obvious that this poetry collection is a very modern one and has recorded what is in the process of happening or what has just happened; it is in sync with life. It can represent part of the traces of modern life. Because of this, the process of translating this book was not difficult for me. But this doesn't mean I didn't encounter problems. For example, the idiom "岁月如梭" literally means "the sun and the moon are like shuttles flying on a loom," but since it is a fixed idiom in Chinese,

I thought we could use a fixed English phrase to express it. Initially I put "how time flies" for the translation. In the end, Zhou Li and I decided to go with the original translation. He wanted its "deeper layer of meaning" to be shown. Similarly, I have tried to remain faithful to the original meaning and mood throughout the book in hopes that you may understand Zhou Li's poems in English as they were originally written.

Xi Nan
July 25, 2020

Preface

Fish Lu: Please tell us about your day job first. Do you like your work? Why did you choose this career?

Zhou Li: My profession is a medical worker. For me, this is just a means to earn my living. It is just a job. I use it to get material things and to support my spiritual life as much as possible. The initial career choice was made by my parents. I always listen to them. I don't like this job. There are too many repressive and helpless things in the state institutions, and extremely rational thinking is needed. But I'm a sentimental person

Fish Lu: Please describe your daily life. Are you satisfied with your current living status?

Zhou Li: If you had asked me more than ten years ago, I would have answered: Satisfied, or dissatisfied. But not anymore. Basically, you have no choice: everyday I go to work, get off work, occasionally write poems, and try my best to live as others do. You need to calmly face the various circumstances in life, whether proactively or passively. It is difficult for us to change anything.

Fish Lu: Why do you think you should "live as others do"? Is it because of the pressure from your surroundings?

Zhou Li: After all, life is trivial. You need to have various relationships with different kinds of people, and you can't isolate yourself from the crowd, so it is better to have some commonality. I'm not exactly afraid of pressure, but I also want to be more relaxed

Fish Lu: What kind of person do you think you are? Do you think other people's impression of you matches yours?

Zhou Li: The opposites of many things coexist in me. For example, I sometimes can be very talkative, while sometimes very quiet, a great contrast. I can only keep looking for the point of unity among contradictions. But this point is constantly changing, so my status is continuously unstable and lacks a sense of security. I'm always worried that accidents will suddenly happen and beautiful things will suddenly disappear. On the spiritual level, it is difficult for me to find people who I can communicate with as equals. I think very few people understand me, and I don't need others to understand either. Loneliness is my normal state. Perhaps most of the people I know still have limited thinking: we are not on the same level of communication.

Fish Lu: So you are a person with fierce internal conflicts. Have you ever thought about the specific sources of these conflicts?

Zhou Li: I believe that a large part of any individual's destiny is actually doomed. This is not philosophical idealism. I think the real reasons are also there, but not as important. My father's early death may be one of the reasons. At that time, I was an adolescent and my core values were budding.

Fish Lu: When, and for what reason, did you start writing poetry? What does writing poetry mean to you?

Zhou Li: I started writing poetry about five or six years ago. There was no special reason. I just started to write one day. Before that, I basically had very little knowledge of modern poetry. Later, maybe because of a girl, I then started to consciously write and showed it to her. She was my entire world. Poetry is the natural outflowing of my emotions, meaning that I still have emotions, I'm still alive.

Fish Lu: You are relatively low-key in my impression, and now I also feel that you are a little pessimistic. Does this have anything to do with your experience?

Zhou Li: Yes, I am a pessimist, like the color black. You don't see any shadow in black. In fact, there is a difference between pessimism and negativity or decadence, but many people see them as the same. My experience is terrible, no need to talk about it.

Fish Lu: Besides writing poems, what other hobbies do you have to fill your spare time?

Zhou Li: I listen to some music. I am a friend of many folk singers and occasionally I write songs, too. My dad was a morally lofty intellectual, and I have his genes. I usually spend a lot of time with flowers, birds, fish and insects. I have nearly a hundred tortoises and a few cats and dogs, and so forth. I feel that it is much more interesting to communicate with them than with humans.

Fish Lu: Wow, a hundred tortoises, this is beyond my imagination. Let's talk about your tortoises. Is it usually troublesome to take care of them? How much time does it take?

Zhou Li: Ha ha, if you wish, you can accompany them all day long, feeding, changing water, taking care of the environment and hatching, and so forth. People who don't have pets may not understand the hardships and happiness in it.

Fish Lu: Where are you from? Do you think the interpersonal or natural environment there has an influence on you? If so, what are the main influences?

Zhou Li: I live in a coastal town in Ningbo (宁波), Zhejiang China. People here live a peaceful and mediocre life. They basically have no influence on me. The only thing that influences me is emotion. I am a faithful slave to emotions.

Fish Lu: Can "a faithful slave to emotions" be understood as, like to immerse yourself in your own world?

Zhou Li: No one would be willing to be a slave, but I know for myself that I can't get rid of my emotions, then maybe I should give myself in. Perhaps it will reward you with a piece of candy occasionally. I am a very self-centered person, but not closed. So emotion is the only way out.

Fish Lu: For you, what is the relationship between writing poetry, or artistic and spiritual pursuits, and your daily life and job? Is it possible for them to be in a compatible and harmonious state?

Zhou Li: Spiritual and material things are inherently intertwined with each other. It is impossible for one to exist without the other. There can be toleration, but that's not harmony. Poems are the body and spirit imprisoned by me. I always have to stay with things that I don't like.

Fish Lu: Are there any poets or artists you like?

Zhou Li: There are a few. For Chinese poets, perhaps Wu Qing (乌青), Ren Hang (任航) and Yang Li (杨黎). For foreign poets, I like Philip Larkin and Charles Bukowski.

Fish Lu: What do you usually talk about when talking with people?

Zhou Li: When talking with different people, my state will fluctuate greatly, and the specific contents will be different too. If he or she has an interesting soul, I will naturally talk about something interesting: poetry, love, politics, worldviews, and the damn life.

Fish Lu: Seems that the topics can be very diverse, and you're a bit cynical. Do the people around you have such an impression, too?

Zhou Li: Yes, they do. There are many things that make me angry. This is a matter of principle. I habitually see the other side of the coin.

Zhou Li's Poems: 2019-2017

2019

A not-so-familiar friend
Suffocated by coal-burning and committed suicide
Female, 28 years old
What she cared for most in her last words
Was her cat
I don't know her pain
Also have no position to express
My grief

The moon is drifting here
Then drifts there
When I look at the moon
It doesn't move
The clouds are drifting here
Then drift there

A cold wave is coming
Heavy snow falls in the surrounding area
This small town near mountains and the sea
Where I live
Stays unswayed
Occasional pieces of snow
Fall only on the roof

After the spring begins
There is more rain
Those underground corpses
Will slowly wake up, too
Every time it rains
I dig into the soil one time
To see to what depth
The rain has infiltrated

I'm holding fifty-two yellow roses
Covered with a layer of white veil
Outside the church
In a corner
Waiting for you to come
The flowers are a bit heavy
Several times
I wanted to put them down

Smoking in front of a breakfast shop
A little girl around five or six years old
Runs over to the opposite lawn
Takes a piss
From time to time she looks at me
The spring rain in March
At this time, keeps falling

You say, you can go in
It's already the fourth day
Today's color is like a mixture of fresh blood
and coffee
Passionate, and with a ripe scent

Recently went downtown
Found that many parking lots were unmanned
This is pretty good
Unmanned mall
Unmanned hospital unmanned crematorium
And then go to the no-man zone for
Unmanned sex

I really want to jump from
This height
For so many years
What I wanted to do
Was never realized

Came out after watching a movie
It was already late at night
Just now there was sleet outdoors
Now only the snow was left
We went through the streets one after the other
With hands put in
Our respective pockets

The fish in the river are swimming around
I'm still far from the river
But there must be many fish in the river
Swimming around
I don't know whether they're
Happy

I'm already ashamed of
Speaking out loneliness
Pedestrians outside the window turn up their collars
In a hurry on their trips
The weather is still cold
I haven't spoken of
Love for long, either

The moonlight makes shadows
Trees have shadows
I am here, love without shadows
Hate without shadows

Don't like wearing a watch
Especially at night time
The pressing tick-tock by my ears
Will make my heart beat faster
Like someone is warmly inviting:
Welcome to
This wonderful hell

I live by the sea
It is a treasured place
Disasters never happened
Only a heavy rain is remembered in 1997
It kept falling for several days and nights
The water poured into the house
Even now
There are clearly visible marks

The city after rain
Stays still
It doesn't fly up along with
The rising water fog

Anti-theft fence is installed
The sun still shines in
Leaves a few shadows
On my body
Makes me look like
Some kind of striped animal

Every time I see beautiful mountains and rivers
I always feel
A cemetery buried there
Right now the cemetery is clean and tidy
Pines and cypresses are ever green
To look from a distance, they are
Beautiful mountains and rivers

If the doomsday earthquake comes at night
Then the world is a
Huge sex bed

A pile of black plants soaked in water–
First use hard fire to boil it up
Then use slow fire to stew for half an hour
It becomes a bowl of wholesome but bitter medicine
These unknown plants
Go down the throat
Into my stomach
Don't know which season is growing
In my body

Carelessly broke a vase
Sharp shattered glass pierced my finger
Strictly speaking
That was not a vase
When I broke it, there was no flower
Only air in it
I'm wearing a raincoat

So it doesn't really matter to me
Whether it is raining
Just one more kind of
Pattering noise
Makes the world not
Sound that silent now

Keep clenching my fist
And then loosen it
Clenching, and then loosen
I didn't catch anything
Didn't lose anything, either

Before bed
I habitually smoke a cigarette on the balcony
On the right there is the road
Occasionally cars pass by
On the left there is the river. I've never seen
A boat
With a juvenile standing in it

One two three
Sleepless night
I'm neither counting stars
Nor counting sheep
I am counting
The dose of medicine that is
Enough to keep me asleep

The downstairs household
They have a yard full of flowers
I use water
To extinguish the cigarette butt
So that I can throw it further
Not to fall
Among the flowers of others

I want to take some medicine but find
The medicine is out
Can't hear the pills hitting the bottle at night
My heart at the moment
Is empty

The bed takes me to the bakery door
The sunshine is bright
Pedestrians passing by all look at me, say:
What a beautiful girl!
They talk while showering on me
Pink bank notes

Watching fishes by a fish pond
A fish is dead
With its white belly facing the sky
Take another look
It's the illusion formed by the light refraction
Light is ever changing
Sometimes it forms a fish, sometimes a human
And sometimes is those
Indescribable things

Inexplicably want to cry
In fact, many things
Have a reason
But we can't
Walk here and there
On the street
Nakedly anyway

Early spring is a bit cold
Some trees haven't yet grown leaves
Two birds on a branch
Are flapping and playing
They are not chirping

A perfume is placed there for a long time
Never opened
I do not know
What kind of fragrance it has
Also lose the chances to
Infatuate with a certain kind

It is raining outside
I get the conclusion
Based on the weather forecast
The app shows
That the probability of rainfall at the moment
Is 100%

Tomb-Sweeping Day, the sunlight is bright
The rain fell the other day
Dried out soon
Sunlight can take away many things
So do you

I see that I killed two big green snakes
I see a pack of black dogs were chained up
I see the newly-peeled bark slowly softening
I see that I am trying hard to join these fragments

When I heard that the *Cathédrale Notre-Dame* was on fire
It was raining at my place
I am far apart from Paris
Water and fire
Are also far apart

To close the window
So that the fallen leaves are not
Blown in by the wind
Just that, in autumn
There isn't only
Wind and fallen leaves

When loosening the soil, dug out an earthworm
The sharp blade had cut it
Into two
They crept nonstop
Crept into the soil again
I heard that after a while
They'd turn into two independent earthworms
And there wouldn't be any
Further connections between them

Ning is getting married
A simple Western wedding
Invites me to attend
I've never been in a church
Only when passing by occasionally
Would raise my head
To look at the top of the steeple
And see if there was a
Crow perched from medieval times

The rain falls into the water
The sun shines on another piece of sunlight
Today I am
Hiding in my own shadow

Light in the underground garage
It is dim
But I can already read the book in hand clearly
Very few people in here
I actually have a kind of
Inexplicably warm feeling

No matter if it is a happy
Or painful moment
She crosses her arms
And puts them on her chest
Forming a
Collapsed crucifix

No sunshine on the balcony
Among the dense and tidy rows of tall buildings
Some are houses
Some are homes
Among those who're walking on the street
Some are people
Some are beasts
I pick up the scissors and cut out
Withered branches and leaves in the flowerpots

Had a nightmare again
I was shouting hard in it
But couldn't make any sound
Why the thorns of the day
Are always
Stuck in the throat late at night

It is not dead yet
In the pool of blood
Continuously twitching
That car has sped away
I watch from a distance
A street cleaner comes
Throws it into
A green trash can

Myself in the mirror is
Transparent and real
Just that all the organs
Have changed direction
Including my
Heart

I wash my own body
Over and over again
Eyes pious
There is a god in the night
I am full of awe
For it

I like you
Also know where you are
But what's the use?
Many years ago
I also saw
Freedom there

I shred the sunshine
Put it into my mouth
A few
Raindrops
Also fall in

All relationships
Originate from love
All politicians
Serve the people

Birds that were born in the winter
Fly over and land on
This summer's shoulder
One bird
Two birds
More and more birds
People walking by don't hear the birds chirping
Only hear
The woods singing

Don't call me a poet
It scares me
I have grown old
Not good enough for beautiful things
And no longer talk about
Love that often
So be it
Full of birds and beasts in my view
Each holding a broom

I like rain
But am seldom in rain
I like you
But seldom hug you

If in a night when
Peach blossoms are bright and beautiful
I open my eyes
Don't know if I would see
One or two peach blossoms
Or countless
Maybe I open my eyes too late
Only see
Darkness

Bees are all over the flowers
Ants walk through the spring
Flying to me

I've watched three movies alone
This month
Stories on the screen
Audience around
And me
Pretty good
Not so lonely
As imagined

That tree grows too fast
Obstructs the sunlight
When chopping it down
I find an abandoned bird's nest
On the crotch of the tree
So strange
For these years
I rarely heard any chirping
In my ears

Next time I won't buy a white car
Although white looks pretty good
When it's clean
It's too easy to get dusty
Even continuous rain-pouring
Wouldn't help
My first car was black
Ruined in
Our car accident

December the 25th
Morning, rainy
A bus stops in front of the red light
On the rear it's written: Her Spring
When the green light is on
I bow my head
Take a bite of
The red apple in hand

Mother's Day
I did not wish mother a happy mother's day
She knows
For these years
I haven't been happy

The road I know gets sick again
Once in a while
It is cut apart
Excavators dig out from it
Reinforced concrete
Unknown pipelines
And then put in other
Reinforced concrete and unknown pipelines
None of them
Are soft

Three o'clock in the afternoon
The sun shines on the lawn to the right
The tortoise is staying still
On the lawn to the left
If I change my position
Then the sunlight is on the lawn to the left
And the tortoise is now crawling towards
The lawn to the right

Strings of grapes
They are green now
In a few days
They will turn purple, then black
And be eaten by someone
Some will fall to the ground
Become sweet jam

When the rain just started
It was not big
I could easily
Walk through the raindrops
Before they fell on me
And raised dust

If you sit still in a car
With windows closed
Rain keeps flowing down the glass
Then the world at the moment is like
A huge water curtain theater
Mass background actors
And a handful of leading players
Are standing on the highest point of the stage

A busy day in the sun
To build a cover
For the ripening grapes
I feel my shoulders burning and sore afterwards
I am used to shade
Feeling somewhat uncomfortable
So much sunlight suddenly pouring down

On the way back
Wind started to blow
More and more black clouds came
Rain also fell down
Not long after
Into your black camisole
Exposing your
Shallow cleavage

I have never seen
Dandelion seeds
Flying
Even if they flew past before my eyes
I wouldn't know
These are dandelion seeds

Unknown weeds
Overgrown on the tomb
Paper flowers
Fall to the ground

The lake water outside the window is moving
Because there is wind
In my eyes
Tears are also moving
There isn't any wind

I did not eat today
Just had two cans of beer
A plate of pistachios
There were many pistachios
With some salt sprinkled on them

I step on withered leaves
They have no bones
But are making sounds like
Bones cracking

I've been enjoying talking to myself
Since I was a child
When I was talking
I was actually carefully listening

A tomao is lying in the plate
Next to the tomato
There are two apples
And at this time, I am on my way to the kitchen
To get a knife

Awakened by a somewhat sad and shrill voice
Listened carefully for a few minutes
Couldn't tell what was happening
Fell asleep soon
When woke up again
The sunlight was dazzling

A fly in the room
Is flying around
Hitting the glass from time to time
It has a golden head in the sunlight
Keeps hitting the glass

The camellias in the yard
Are opening petals one after another
Spring will be very long
For now I won't
Think of how they will look
When the petals wither
One after another

In the dark night, all light
Is invaders

My naked shell curls up in the blanket
My clothes and my soul
Are hanging on the clothes rack
From time to time
They sway

I bow down
Sip the spring water from the mountain stream
Birds' chirping comes to my ears
The moonlight shines on your nude body

That room is
Different from the other rooms
It has dark red curtains
They are almost never opened
One day they finally opened a little
Oozing in some light

Pick up a fallen leaf
Use half of it
To cover my eyes

Tourists are packed in the park
I am holding a book
Walking through the crowds
The wind opens the book
Making rustling sounds

Mist around the streetlamp
Forms a light halo
It just rained in this early autumn night
A bit cold
Tell me, does this view
Look like winter

I've been lying on the sofa in the living room
The entire day
The bamboo mat from summer is still out
Today's weather is pretty good
Except for warmth
Nothing is left on it

The apartment corridor is equipped with
A row of voice-activated lights
Above them it is a layer of glass
I raise my head
Continuously walk round
This way
The starry sky won't go off

Right after opening the door
Sunlight followed into the house
I quickly closed the door
What I need is
Just an empty house

Many leaves are floating on the creek
Their colors are dark and light
Maybe have fallen down
At different moments
They just float on the water like this
Wherever the water goes
They go with it

So winter comes
Finally I can put on that
Black down jacket
I flap my arms hard
In the cold wind
Imagining I am
A flying angel

Sky is grey
Sea is blue
I leave home
To go to free
A captive fish

How to describe the fallen leaves in the wind
Trembling, struggling
Like at the moment of orgasm of our
Involuntarily
Convulsing bodies

I desperately cover my ears
The sound of rain is getting fainter
The crying sound is getting louder and louder

That red leaf
Suddenly falls to the windshield
I brake the car sharply
It falls down right in front of my eyes
The sunset at this time
Is shining on the river

I'm cutting my left wrist
Very carefully
To guarantee that the power of each cutting is
Just right to tear the skin
Let it seep bright blood drops
Instead of
Mutilating it into a pulp

I want to jump into a
River that is broad enough
Let the body rot
Let my loneliness permeate the whole river
And every thirsty passerby
Will become as lonely
As me

Today we have this year's
First snow
Want to go out and have some food
But I'm afraid of
The coldness outside
If you want the warmth
Then do not go out

I haven't actually seen a crow
Just repeatedly read about it
In books
As time passes
A kind of mysterious religious feeling is formed
I know I won't
See you and a crow
At the same time

The indoor temperature is eight degrees Celsius
Three degrees outside
Ten degrees below the thick leaves
My body temperature is thirty-seven degrees
No fever

Often feel dizzy in recent days
It comes and goes, like ocean waves
When the waves overturned that boat by the beach
Ah—I
Finally throw up

I wear that black dust coat
Occasionally change
The inside shirt
If I don't talk
No one knows that
I have two identical
Black dust coats

You sent some tea leaves from afar
I brew some up
In this humid and cold weather
Stir it gently with a spoon
Producing a vortex
The little vortex
Makes me
Want to jump in

We haven't seen each other for long
You say, yes
The weather is too cold
And women are made of water
Will freeze
You take off the black coat
While talking
Showing your rainbow-colored sweater

Cloudy day, light rain
I bought an axe online
Recently there's always something
Flashing in my head

Today there is sunshine
Really rare
I mean it is rare that
I am in a good mood
And this has little to do
With the sunshine

For some places
It is impossible to go back again
Like Huoxian Town
Like paradise
Thinking of those times in Huoxian
Feels just like paradise

Winter
Leaves fall
Hair grows long
Walk out after the haircut
Remember an important thing
I should wear a warm hat
So that my bare veins
Do not cramp
In cold nights

Near the end of the funeral
Firecrackers
Are set off
In the sound of firecrackers
A black wild cat jumps out
From nowhere
Staring at me
On its chest
There's a white crescent

What can I do
On this gloomy afternoon
The world is constantly repeating itself
On the west-facing balcony
One bird after another
Flies back to the nest
One after another
Car
Runs by the zebra crossing

I called Little Huang
It then
Runs to me
Lying on its belly
In both of our eyes
There is a moon
They're both very kind
Christmas Eve
Dreamed that I had
Received a lot of
Red apples
I took a bite
Of
Each of them

Tear off the hangnail on the ring finger
Paint on red
Nail polish
I watch the wound
Become a solid blood scab
My gaze slowly
Becomes softer

The first time I woke up
It was one o'clock in the morning
Still far from the dawn
Drank a cup of coffee
Wanted to put some sugar in it
Didn't find any

We've talked a lot
Work, life
Helpless confusions
And at this moment
The weather outside
We
Coincidentally
Did not talk about love

It is bitterly cold
I put a hot water bottle
Between my two legs
It is a rose-colored hot water bottle
What needs to be warmed in winter
It is not the heart
But the desire

You want to have a cat
Black
Not the kind in pet shops
Those docile cats
I think about it—
Let's go tramping then
Tramps
Will meet
Tramping cats

The cold in the south is everywhere
Whether it's the living room
Kitchen, bathroom
Or the single bed
The cold in the south
Is everywhere, like your
Love

You want to eat grilled fish
I take you to eat
Freshly killed fish
With all kinds of pretty spices
The iron plate is emitting white steam
Accidentally eat a wild pepper
Mouth feeling needled
Take a look at you opposite
My heart is needled, too

The rain and the glass window
Having been talking
The sound is sometimes loud, sometimes small
This evening
The rain has also talked with
Many people

Want to drink watermelon juice
So I make a glass myself
I put the green peel
Black seeds
And red pulp
All in
Red fruit juice is produced
The green and the black
Are unrecognizable

I like raising some
Flowers, birds, fish and insects
They don't speak
I think we are
Alike
Actually they can also speak
Just that I
Couldn't understand

I didn't go in
Because I was afraid
My wet-look
Would make your heart ache
You knew that I wouldn't bring an umbrella
And you saw
It was raining outside the window

I know smoking is not good
Just that the empty feeling in my hands
Will make me uneasy
I also see that
Many years later
On a windy and snowy night in Yan Village
A dying patient of chronic bronchitis
Struggling to sit up
Trying hard to cough out
The long-held bubbles in their chest

A lot of rain in the south of the
Yangtze River in winter
Heavy rain, medium rain
Small rain
Continuously raining
Every drop falls on the ground
The world does not need too many sceneries
As long as there is rain
If there is also, you,
Would be perfect

You put on bright lipstick
I eat it
Slowly, slowly
Rouge D Armani Matte Lipstick New Year's Premiere
Red lips ignite your colorful life
Baby, Happy New Year

2018

I keep flicking cigarette ashes
The red firing butt
Is like a bloodshot glans
Lighting up
My future road

Time is the best remedy
To forget a person
In the next life
I could then forget you

When the failed marriage
Is over, colleague Li
Cut her beautiful phoenix eyes
Into double eyelids
Does she have to make one more wound
Upon the original wound
So that to see the world
More clearly

Estazolam
Clonazepam
Alprazolam
A bunch of antidepressant medicines
Are on the desk
My heart
Feels more and more uneasy

The midnight cello sound
Is like a blunt knife
Cutting my throat
Back and forth
At this time
The snow
Is also
Pouring down

Mom says
Dad and her
Often looked at me and my elder sister sleeping
"Look, how beautiful our children are"
I guess
Then they'd certainly
Kissed each other
More than once

The fish on the table
Its body has been eaten
Revealing the white skeleton
Nobody cares about
The fish head with the open mouth

The sun and the moon
Are like shuttles flying on a loom
I count for goddamn nothing

A patient of diabetes ketoacidosis
Is in a coma in bed
Full of pipes on his body
His urine sugar
Blood sugar
Organs all over his body
Are full of sugar
He will die in sweetness

In the packed Great Compassion Shrine
My hand accidentally touched the soft breast
Of a passing girl
Some nasty thoughts just emerged
I looked up and saw the bodhisattva
Startled
Quickly knelt down

Many years later
Come to Tiantong Temple again
Maybe because it's now winter
See no sign of life
In the outdoor Free Life Pond[1]
I don't have the desire
To jump in, either

Open the curtain a little bit
Looking at the outside dark night
It's a little bit blacker
Than the inside

The light in a window is on
After the light in another window goes off
Things happen by accident
But you want to find
Some poetic meaning in them

If the rain slowly falls down
Then it is like
Flowing down
Wherever it flows
It turns into liquid
And my body is also
Slowly softened

She is wearing a yellow dress
Extremely Beautiful
As if the skin would break
By being only blown or touched
Like a just-hatched chick
From the spring
I'm thinking
How to eat her
Salted chicken, drunken chicken
Or cold boiled chicken
Or to be primitive
Just swallow her with hair and blood

The wind blows across the boundless prairie
Blows over the flocks of
Cows and horses
Turns a corner
Blows to me

I'm on your body
Very lightly
Like a fallen leaf is
Upon another fallen leaf

The motherland is in my heart
The Party is in my heart
The leaders are in my heart
I can only
Move myself out

The fetus just came to this world
The midwife with scissors
In her hand
Cuts the umbilical cord
Instantly the kin is separated

A donkey covered with a piece of red silk
Wanders into an unfinished construction
Braying nonstop
The scream passes from the east wall to the north wall
From the north wall to the west wall
Not yet reaching the south Wall
It stops braying

I pick up the freshly fallen ginkgo leaves
Piece by piece
Want to use them to cover all over my yard
Passers-by
They look at the fallen leaves
Then look at me

I can't tell this moment—
Is it early morning or dusk
The blood-red sun is stuck on the horizon
Neither rising
Nor falling

A sudden power failure
No pre-sign
Everything disappears
Including the light in my wife's eyes
We are silent to each other
Seem to get used to
This charming blackness for long

A peach tree is planted
In the yard of our house
Mother says
This makes it easy to attract luck with women
We should chop it down
Father died young
I always listen to mother
That peach tree's just recently bloomed
Not yet borne fruit

She is thinking
Whether to embroider a flower
On this fine silk
Hesitates for a moment
She gives up
Because without this flower
The silk is already very beautiful

Snow falls
On the frosty roof
After becoming hopeless for freedom
I believe in love again

If there is a train coming from behind
And you can't run faster than it
You can only
Choose to leave the original track
And on another track
You're waiting for another
Train to come

A match in the dark night
Dropped to the ground
In some corner
I used up all the remaining matches
To find it
Hesitating if I wanted to
Use it
To ignite the dark night

I bite gently
I like your softness and stickiness
Dare not bite hard
I'm afraid if it's broken
It will reveal
The black stuffing

When brushing my teeth
Looking at the mirror
My mouth is full of white foams
Which I really like

I actually had physiological reactions
When examining the girl's body
And I found
Myself to be a vulgar guy
This discovery
Made me rapturous

At the wedding
They should light more firecrackers
Lest the funeral
Should have no one to appreciate

A rag is not necessarily for table-wiping
If when you're wiping a table
Thinking of something and cry
You could also use the rag
To wipe tears

Darling
Without you I will
Die
You've never believed me
Including the words
I've just said

I want to sleep in the rain tomorrow night
I am a doctor
So no need to worry too much
Red green yellow
Sugar-coated tablets dispersible tablets
sustained-release tablets
I have everything
Then
Only rain is missed

Lovers are holding flowers
Opening their hearts on Valentine's evening
Neon is red, Wine is green
Genitals in the night
Are glinting

The night in Starbucks
Almost ten o'clock
You're still sitting by the window
Working hard
For the coming event
I can't be of any help
Just sometimes look at you
Sometimes look at the moon
I've also just checked
Tomorrow's rain

My motherland is a huge plastic wrap
I am forever an immortal flower inside

For two continuous days
When I got home late at night
A cat jumped out of the trash can at the door
Escaped in panic
Both of the times
It escaped in the same direction
I saw that cat
It was as black
As the dark night

It is time to make a change
This noon
I want to cook tomatoes
With hen eggs
Instead of
Duck eggs

I want to grow something like
Japanese banana or Chinese parasol tree
In the yard
This way when rain drops on them
There will be
Some sounds

In Starbucks I've only drunk
Milk and Latte
Oh, that day
I also tried some mousse cake for free
And you waved your hand
Said you didn't want any

Today, June 4th
An ordinary day
Sunny
But not strong

Heavy snow like goose feathers
Is falling from the sky
Thinking that so many geese are defeathered
I feel so sad

The snow is flying down
In profusion
Flying down
In profusion
Black men
Turn white
White men
Disappear

I was born in the
Warm amniotic fluid
Died in a raging fire
Between life and death
Have been living
An incompatible life
As fire and water

Remember going to Beijing many years ago
Loitering on Wangwangjing Street
In that extremely cold winter
Among the bushes whose leaves had all fallen
Various flowers were blooming
Take a closer look
They were plastic flowers
This is not as good as the south
Even when it's very cold weather
There are always some real colors
Blooming

Miss Spring
Miss Spring
It is so cold
I really want to sleep with you

I say oh baby
You have to eat well and rest well
Do take care
Take care
This city is too pompous
Too light
Like it's flying away any minute

A crow should
Have been born from within the horse leather[2]
Carrying a bone of the dead in its mouth
Flies over the blue ocean
And stops behind the neon lights
Above the top of a
Church
Hovers in the wind
That is
A true crow

I'm lying on the bamboo recliner
The recliner is in the courtyard
The courtyard
Is under the sun
I squint
The wind by my ears
Tells me:
Spring is here

Completely frozen yesterday
But today it's twenty degrees
Going to rain in just a few days
And next week
New cold air is coming again
I keep adjusting
Clothes hat umbrella
And my worldview...
To adapt to
God's bad temper

There will be rain tomorrow morning
I want to wait for it
From tonight

It takes about
Two to three minutes
To finish a cigarette
But if you stand and smoke in the wind
That's not necessarily the case
It depends on
The direction of the wind

Recently been waking up in the middle of the night
Open my eyes
Sometimes see darkness
Sometimes light grey air
Sometimes the vague dawn
And if I'm lucky
Can even hear a
Continuous rain

In a dream last night
There was a green train[3]
There was you and me
So
That was a perfect dream

I'm watching an ant moving
A grain of rice
The rice is full and firm
The ant's moving with a lot of effort
The sun is too scorching
Hasn't yet reached home
The rice has already become
Popcorn

To describe the exciting waves in the heart
Of people in love
With the feeling of "electric shock"
Is very inaccurate
Love is more like
Boiling a frog in warm water
Later the frog dies without foreseeing
And the water gets cold

Do not lament the twists and turns in life
When you die
Your cardiogram will become
A straight line
Between two points
The shortest distance is
A straight line

A brilliant "Trash School" poet
Comes to visit me
He was born in the 1980s
Looks old though
Talking about his former girlfriend while chatting
Her name is "Dust"
He says he still can't forget her

Around seven o'clock in the morning
Go out to deal with something
Although the weather is sunny
Still
Feels cold
I habitually shake my body
Accidentally
Also shake off
The sunlight that has
Just landed on my shoulders

Inadvertently feel
The smell of my fingers
And remember
Yesterday
Carefully peeled off a red orange
Ate it
The pulp was red and juicy
I then remember a long time ago
I carefully
Stripped off your clothes

Separated by a piece of glass
I
Cry out for help
Exhaling
Only an expanse of water vapor
Others can't see me
I can't see
Others, either

The signboard of Minsheng Bank
Is glinting
In the dark
But no beggar or
Tramp
Walks pass by the glint
This makes me
A little disappointed

Another construction worker
Fell down
From a scaffolding
Died
Every time a festival comes
There seems to be so many such things
The higher the floor is
The easier he dies

Wine makes my heart beat faster
Transfers heat to the capillaries
In the superficial body parts
Make me flush in the face
Body heats
Only an expanse of desolation
Is left in the heart

Move to the left
To the right
Upward, downward
The bigger the bed is
The harder I could fall asleep

Taking the subway late at night
Only yourself
In the whole carriage
You will then think
At the next stop
Will there be
A human
Coming in

The stone lion on the bridge
Surfaces
From the water
Again
It sinks and emerges
Sometimes hidden
Sometimes visible

Wake up from a nightmare
Sweat all over the body
Licking the salty taste
And remembering myself
Is an expanse of ocean

The reading lamp
On the night table right hand side
Has been on all this time
But I
Habitually turn my back to it—
To the light

There's wind on the hill
Let's go and collect it

Today I've been in bed the whole time
Only drank some of the white milk
That has already been expired for ten days
This is to say, expired things
Are still
Of some use
In a while

There is a
Trapped fly
On the spider web
But it's not eaten
I am thinking
What is wrong with
The spider

Death is a stream of smoke
Very light and thin
I swallowed it
But it comes out again
From the nostrils

A colleague from the Obstetrics
And Gynecology Department
Tells me a true story:
A boy took a photo
Of the almond-shape flesh
That was just aborted
From the girl's body
And posted it on his social media
While grinning

It took 99 steps from the south to the north
But took 100 steps from
The north to the south
The same journey
Just in different directions
I am thinking
Which step
Was wrong

Several workers are trimming trees
With a chainsaw
Chopped-off branches
Are scattered on the ground
Some walk by
Trees and people
Are all very calm

There's a babel of voices
In front of the food market
It's like a pot of congee
Being cooked in my head

People tightly embracing on Valentine's Day—
Their ashes after death
Will be placed separately

I am a patient of high myopia
Thick glasses
Separate me
From the world

Do you like me
I do
Which kind of like
Actually there's only
One kind of like
But there are many different kinds of
Endings

Blue sky
White sun
Red leaves all over the field
I admit that at this moment
I am
Free

Last night father
Called my name in my ear
I heard it very clearly
Thinking in a trance that
After the Spring Festival
I will be forty-three years old
Exactly the same age
When he died

Hear late at night
Outside the monitor room, cats are screaming
Along with the sound of
Garbage cans falling to the ground
Can't help checking it out
Open the door
My eyes meet the eyes of two mating cats
The atmosphere suddenly
Becomes a bit awkward

After the vernal equinox
It will soon be the Tomb-Sweeping Day
Spring diverges from here
Two roads
One to life
One to death

I am a vegetarian
Don't eat beef lamb and pork
Only eat greens cabbage carrots
Be a
Colorful plant
And then be eaten by
Girls full of flesh and blood

Spit out the grape skins
When eating grapes
Spit out the bones when eating meat
I eat the moon
And spit out the dark night

To open a door
No matter if it's
Of a new house
Or an old courtyard
A proper key is needed
While closing the door
Only
Myself alone
Is needed

Even during the day
This village among the hills
Is very quiet
When night becomes darker
Gradually there are more
Sounds
Some people come, some people leave
Some are walking back and forth

I used to like the dark night so much
Silky blackness
Fascinating
But now prefer to light a lamp
I get more and more worried that
The dark night
Is a huge scabbard
Will absorb away all my
Light

Golden small flowers are
All over the hill
I pick one
Don't really want to
Put it in your hair
I want to plant it
Between your legs
And see
Which flower is more beautiful

I was killed again and again
In various ways
After waking up
Only remember
The director and actor
Were all myself
And those murderers–
I can't remember any of them

Xu Huan is a designer
Has a comely face
She's the kind of girl with small breasts
Which I like
She wears a white-horse earring
On her left ear
Swings
Along with the body and wind
She is from Hubei Province
A place called Angel Town

Me and you are in the restaurant
It is raining outside
A young man and a young woman
Pass by
One with an umbrella
One without
I can't tell if they are a couple
The rain's not heavy
Just enough to get people wet

I'm eating you in bed
The "flower cakes" delivered
Taste ok
Just that I wouldn't
Associate them with flowers
If comparing you to
A flower
Then
It makes much more sense

You say in this autumn
I look very good
In a shirt
I say
You look even better than autumn
I am a fickle person
In the spring last year
I once said
You look even better than spring

Spring and autumn are a pair of twins
Have similar temperature
Usually more than ten or twenty degrees
But they have different endings
One runs into blaze
The other
Integrates into coldness

A bird is flying in the sky
The next day
That bird is still flying in the sky

A gust of autumn wind blows over
The autumn wind
Blows from the south to the north
Some leaves
Fall in front of my eyes
Rustling
There're also leaves falling not far away
But the sounds can't be heard

An ambulance drives by at night
Speedily
An unknown patient is lying in it
It's already winter
The dazzling headlights
Are shining on one tree
After another
Those bare trees
Move backwards

I see dust
Is purple
The sunlight slanting down
Some dust
Dances under it
When tired
On that violet pajama
They sleep for a while

Ningbo at 3:13 in the morning
Is colorful
Some streetlights are white
Some streetlights are yellow
Red lights are red
Green lights are green
Where the lights do not shine
Are black

2017

Recently I have a bad appetite
Don't want to eat
But that pretty waitress
Brings me a full bowl of rice
Hemispherically bulges
White and tender
Like her young breasts
Suddenly stimulates some of my desires

So natural
Dreamed about you again
I am on the high hill
You, across the river
Fall asleep facing me
Your white bra
Is laced
Once in a while
A ray of light
Shines on your body

Today that patient
Comes again to prescribe sleeping pills
He cannot live without this medicine
I cannot live without you
This is not a poem
This is just a
Mental prescription

It only took a short while
For you to fall asleep
I can see that
You are a bit tired
I want to touch your face
But take my hand back
In the air
I draw a cross

After the new leader came
The decoration never stopped
Every day at my workplace
It's like being on a noisy stage
A crappy metal band
Thinks their
Every drumbeat
Exactly hits
The G spot of the epoch

Open a bottle of beer
Open another bottle
The beers are opened one after another
I don't plan
To drink them
I'm just looking at
The blooming frothy foam
Among it will there suddenly appear
The Kwan-yin Bodhisattva[4]

It is stormy outside
A flock of birds in the tree by the door
Is chirping
The whole night long
Like people who can't buy a ticket home
Are loudly grumbling

This movie is very good
Every picture
Is full of texture
Near the end of the screening
People get up one after another
In the huge cinema
I still sit
Waiting for the ending song to sound
Waiting for my romantic feeling
To slowly perish

The blanket is short
Cover the head
Then the feet are uncovered
Cover the feet
Then the head is uncovered
I'm a righteous person
Can't curl up to sleep
So before the dawn comes
I die of the cold

Sometimes
I
Am in a good mood
A white crow is chirping
When daybreak comes
There should be someone
Asleep

Close the door
And close the window
Block all the gaps
Lights off
People always need to get used to
Growing old together with
The things you don't love

Walking to Tiananmen Square
The spring breeze coming into my face
Makes me uneasy
So take off the high heels
And change to that pair of
White embroidered shoes
Gently walk every step—
I'm afraid of waking up
The baby sleeping underground

Every straw
Is a hope
Every hope
Is always a straw

The spring is in the city
Flowers are flying everywhere
Dead flowers are
For the dead
Fresh flowers are
On the tall trees
Unreachable

I removed several withered petals on the outer layer
The rose was back to life
After a few days
Removed some more
In the end, only a bare stem was left
I inserted it into the soil
Hoping to gain some same flowers
The flower was gifted from you
A pink half-blooming rose

A friend travels to Xiamen
After enough food and alcohol
Some lust is understandable
He sends me a picture
Says this one is good
Whole night costs a thousand and three hundred yuan
That prostitute has a beautiful look and delicate eyes
Wearing a floral cotton-padded jacket
If we go back to the Republic of China
She might wear an openwork cheongsam
Let's not fuck
Just sing a Li Sao[5]

In dreams
I can always write good poems
Even
Great poems
When the daybreak comes
Poems are gone
And life is here

A group of People's Police
Took advantage of the night
Swooped the red-light district in the east of the city
A new round of anti-porn actions kicked off
Naked erotic men and women
In front of the white dazzling flashes
Were covering their faces
Abandoning
Their trembling bodies

Going through the security check at the airport
A staff member took my travel bag and asked
What's inside
So heavy
Books, they're all books
He glanced at me
Put the bag onto the conveyor belt
To accept a further scan
At the same time
I also quickly passed the security gate
At the sound of the siren
Stopped
Raised my both hands

A retired obstetrician
Says while chatting that
When she was still at work
There were several induced labor cases every day
One case was deeply impressive
That little boy
Flopped about for quite a while
Before he died
What a pity
She gestures with her hands
His birdie was already this long

That young man
Jumped off from the eighteenth floor
When sent to the hospital
He was almost dead
Breathing while nodding
He kept nodding
Seemed to be very satisfied by
The flight this time

Click-clack, click-clack
A lazy sound follows me
On this rainy early morning
Exceptionally clear
Until that sound
Turns into the ladies toilet
And disappears in a burst of
Louder sound

On top of my corpse
Pave a layer of golden leaves—fall
This is so good
Even though I no longer open my eyes
I won't feel it
Dark around

Good night, sometimes means
I miss you
Sometimes
Just to tell myself
A long night is coming

If the plane explodes in the air
Fragments of my limbs
May spread towards
Anywhere in the 9.6 million square kilometers of land
One sharp bone
Inserted into the
Throat of one flying bird

The wind was blowing all night long
Before the daybreak
Finally pried a little slit
Beside the window
The carefully planned tomb robber
Was so disappointed
Didn't see any gold or silver treasure
But only
One imitation mummy

Babe
Be good
You're asleep
Then sleep well
Don't walk around
In my dream

There is no free lunch
In the world
I thought about this question for the whole day
Why not breakfast
Why not dinner
Afternoon tea would also be ok
Thought about it for quite some time
Still don't get it

Having switched off the phone for 24 hours
Restarted
No one says good night
There's only a gust of
The sound of continual pattering raindrops

If it hadn't been interrupted by the knock on the door
The development of things
Was as I wished—
We just slipped into the blanket
Loneliness was like a fire
Darling, do not hurry
Let me look at you
It is impossible for us to
Step into the same river
Not to mention it's a river in the dream

A flood
Washed down the Dragon King Temple on the mountain
It also washed away
Among "Serve the People"
Written on the town government wall
The word "People"
The old people can no longer be found
And the new people are
Waiting for the next flood

The reason why I sleep naked
Maybe that
I don't want my mother
To be too sad
Because
When she first saw me
I was in my
Stark nakedness

In the eyes of others
I am an arrogant person
When seeing the leaders
Become neither too humble nor too polite
They do not know
I've been sick since I was sensible—
Lumbar intervertebral disc protrusion
Having this disease
If I only bend over slightly
It hurts

A hedge in between keeps friendship ever green
When I say goodbye to you
Tears are in the corners of my eyes
If you see them
And kiss them
It tastes salty
Darling
We are not friends
We are lovers

Every first and fifteenth day of lunar month
Mother worships the bodhisattva
Muttering something in her mouth
The reason why I am still alive
Probably because of this
Mama
What should I do if you die
You know that
I've never believed in anything

Red scarf is
Dyed with fresh blood on white cloth
I am very convinced to that
On Children's Day
I bought a red scarf
Chewed it in my mouth
Chewed for three days and nights
It is true that blood of various colors
Flew out from my mouth

Today some senior leaders
Will come to our hospital for inspection
In the meeting room, full of
Exquisite fruit
Some flies are flying
Seeking the right opportunities
For them
All this
Is no different from shit

On the huge billboard
"China Dream" is written
Under the billboard
A beggar is sleeping on the ground
I dare not toss a coin to him
I'm afraid the sound
Would interrupt
His dream

Early morning
Awakened by the sound of firecrackers
Should be another happy event
Not sure if it is
Red
Or white[6]
I close my eyes
The sound of firecrackers continues
I can't tell
Any of its emotions

Poplars by the road
Are tall and straight
They've kept this posture
For many years
But still
They've not pierced the sky
Always there're gardeners who receive instructions
To cut those
Upward branches

After the storm
There will always be leaves falling
Some yellow
Some fresh green
Those half-dead ones
Are me

At the last second of yesterday
I was trying to
Smoke a cigarette. No
Maybe it was
The first second of tomorrow
At the moment when
The match was lit against the black phosphor
I heard
The pendulum in the church
Oscillated a bit

Grandma passed away
Face pale
Like a piece of thin paper
Returned from the burial
I thought that
After all, paper
Couldn't cover fire

I don't like snow
The southern snow is
Often not so thorough
It doodles the world
Into expanses of black and white
I'm up in the air
Watching the chessboard silently

I think the coolest thing
I've ever done is that
When facing the temptation of a pretty girl
I responded like this:
I like making love
Not mating.
Although regretted for many days
At that time
I felt I was like
A noble

On the tactile paths of this city
I've never seen
A blind man
More healthy people
Walk on them
They do not know
Which side is
The east

Most often
I stand in front of the trash can of the city
Feeling this is
Where I belong
Just hesitate
Between
Recyclable and non-recyclable

On the computer it shows one after another
Names of the patients to be diagnosed
If there is no surprise
The same names
Will appear on their tombstones
Thinking about this
I feel my job has
Not much meaning

I push away the cremation worker
No!
This is too painful
I got to live
I'm defeated and flee
Steaming all over my body
People on the roadside are in small groups
Talking about the harvest this year
Crops are ripe
It's time to reap

The person who jumps off the building
In midair
Repents

For an apple
Or pear
If it goes bad
It will rot
Then disappear
If one person goes bad
He might live better

Winter morning
I bought a Chinese twisted cruller and a flatbread
Eating them while walking
The wind wraps me from all directions
Pushing me forward
I glance back
The crowd behind
Are all covered with water fog

I've already counted countless sheep
Still can't fall asleep
Streetlamps
Go out at five in the morning
The Godot I've been waiting for
Did not show up
Time to get up
Oh, also to put on
The whole night scenery

That bird
Is still motionless
The rain at twelve o'clock
Also seems to have no difference
With it at zero o'clock

The local custom:
To be the first in cremation of the day
After death
Is more auspicious
Commonly known as "the first cremation"
Family members of the deceased
Covered with snot and tears on their face
Scrambling
To put the body of their loved one
Into the fire pit

Fish sees through the human trick
Eats up all the bait
Burps and swaggers away
People on the bank
Staring at the increasing bubbles
Looking forward to surprises

Only the lights in the massage shop
Are still on
Some sexy women inside
Are walking back and forth
Finally I want to push the door and enter
A moth was
Quicker than me
To knock on the door

Clean my body
Cut it into small pieces
Put them on the firewood
Together with rice, oil and salt
Potassium sorbate
Formalin
And my ideology
Make them into cans
And send to the shelves of major supermarkets
Put on price labels

Use my books
To build a
Space
Based on a non-linear language
It's about 1.8 meters long
60 centimeters high
40 centimeters wide

The one book in the southeast corner
Will be given to you
So that wind
Can blow in

The friend on the phone
Can't stop crying
The grandma who had loved her, passed away
But she doesn't have enough money
To go back home
She is a poor person
Homeless
Once sent me a photo
That was in a satiny desert
A bird was
Wrapped in a kasaya

Before my father died
There was gurgling in his throat
Medically speaking
That was due to respiratory muscle weakness
And caused sputum accumulation
But I prefer
To believe
That is a lotus

So many books in the bookstore
Have some
Never been opened
By anyone
Some were once opened
Dust fell
And then closed

I really envy
Those plants
In broad daylight
They can make love with
Their lovers at a distance

Whenever it rains
I mean the kind of rain that goes on and off
Always there're in the department
All kinds of umbrellas
Left there by patients
I stare at them
Trying to guess
What their owner is like

Someone sat down on the empty seat next to me
From the beginning to the end
I did not look at him
He did not look at me, either

Rainy day
People are holding umbrellas
Like holding one after another
Moving graves

I am not a cowardly person
I also want to
Seize the neck of fate
But fate is one step ahead
Seized
My neck

The waitress asks:
Sir
Any drink for you?
Boiling water with ice please
Isn't that just a glass of warm water?
She looks surprised
No
That's different

I've never seen a red-crowned crane in reality
That day
You ran to me
Elegantly
Wearing a bright red hat
The sunshine at five o'clock
Just happened to stop on
The ends of your hair

Since I'd drunk too much alcohol
I went to bed earlier than usual
Wake up
And hear the sporadic sounds of firecrackers
Then vaguely remember
Today's already in the New Year
Come to the window
Push open
A nightingale has glided across the night
Flies to somewhere unknown

The poems of Anna Akhmatova
Are nothing too special
I am not an arrogant person
But in my opinion
Life is nothing too special, either

If I fail to write any poem in a few days
That doesn't affect my mood
I believe
It will come to me
But not seeing you for a few days
I feel inexplicable fear
That kind of fear—
Is it called "love"?

I once had a blind date without telling my parents
That was a nurse
Very beautiful
Due to various reasons
The relationship was cut off as soon as it sprouted
She was a determined Christian
When I was crying and desperate to see God
She hugged me
Softly said:
Amen!

I have an umbrella
A black oiled paper umbrella with a long handle
I rarely use it
Usually I wait for the rain to stop
Or turn lighter to walk out
The umbrella was gifted from you
On a sunny afternoon
It wasn't raining on the day

Any mind exchanges without body communication
Are immoral
I am a noble person
But retain vulgar interests
The hand I stretch out to you
Is not a hand of friendship
I'm here to play erotic

The current election method in villages
Is pretty good
Village leader-candidates
Go door by door to say flattering words
And give out some small gifts
I am thinking
If one day
The Mayor, County Mayor, Governor of the province
And even the Chairman of the country
All queue up to my house
Then I will make a good fortune!

The law is really terrible
It splits my mother
My elder sister
And me
Into three households

For another time
He slaps the door and walks out
He is sick of everyday
Without love or making love
Only endless quarrels left
Calm down
Calm down for a while
Find a thorough way to end it all
Before twilight comes
He is back
With a brand new kitchen knife
The tip of the knife is glinting
He promised a few days ago
To cook a meal
For the children in the evening

In the park
Children are chasing each other
Blowing soap bubbles
There's one particularly beautiful
Big
Floating above the heads of a couple taking wedding photos
Stays there for a few seconds
Suddenly breaks

Sometimes suddenly think of an inspiration
I will write it down
If there is no paper or pen
Then record it on the cell phone
Sometimes too lazy to record
Then forget
Thinking of this inspiration occasionally after a long time
Found that I already
Don't like it anymore

A new story encourages marriage and giving birth
In my hometown:
When my cousin got married
Paid a deposit of six-thousand yuan
First baby will get a three-thousand refund
Second baby will get another three-thousand refund

Ever since becoming a colloquial poet
I turned less lyrical
For example, if I can't meet you
I would say
I feel a little bit bad
This is far less sorrowful and literary
Than saying
Ten thousand arrows shooting through my heart

My wife's been infertile for many years
On the pregnancy test kit
There are now two striking red strips
This is an unlucky color
The birth of life
Should be accompanied by blue
Starry blue

A new noodle shop is opened opposite my workplace
Closes very late
The owner is a female
In her thirties
We become familiar after a few visits
Talk about each other
Make some dirty jokes
Sometimes in the hungry nights
I imagine that amorous lady boss
To comfort
My body

Alcohol is really a good thing
Many years ago I killed a crucian carp
It struggled hard
Slipped onto the ground several times
Later I used a white cloth
To cover its eyes
And poured some wine on the cloth
As expected it stopped struggling
Let me do whatever I wanted
Now I sometimes use this method
To deal with myself
But it doesn't work

Ghosts of the Hades
Should also spend the Spring Festival
I went to the graveyard at night
Stayed for a while
The phosphorus fire tonight
Was particularly gorgeous
I just watched it like this
Forgot that in the world behind me
There were also fireworks

Using foggy weather
For dating
Is the most suitable
We can feel each other's beauty
While not clearly seeing
The other's details

Rain is coming
Some unknown birds
Are flying close to the ground
Screaming
I'm on the balcony on the 25th floor
Looking down on these birds
Which once made me envious

You didn't talk to me for a few days
Know that you are engaged
And busy
Dare not disturb you
I can only send messages to some familiar or strange people
Sorry
I can't find anyone to talk to

Passing by a playground
Freshmen are in military training
The sun is scorching in September
The drill master's words
Are sharp, powerful
Like a bamboo stick
Stringing them together
Oozing roasted sizzling oil

At that time you were training at Ningbo University
I went to see you
It was snowing outside the window
I said let's go for a walk
Nope
It's cold outside
Snowflakes will wet our hair
The snow stopped the next day
I still have some regrets now
If I insisted
We could grow old together
Overnight

After going to the toilet
Lift pants
Turn around
Flush
Piously watch
A part from my body
Disappearing instantly
Into the dark vortex

This year's climate is unusual
Should be the coldest season of the year
It's now warm as spring
Sometimes there's thunder
And rain
I am alert
To this phenomenon
I should still wear a heavy down jacket
Perhaps the coldness will
Arrive as expected

After showering
Looking at the mirror
Inside there's a wet water ghost
Also looking at me

There are eight birds
I count again
It is exactly eight
Jumping in the grass
From time to time, using their pointed bill
To kiss the earth
Under the tree a dozen meters away
I am smoking
And watching them
A glob of bird poop suddenly falls on
The red cigarette butt
Makes my poetic feeling disappear
And in front of my eyes
Only one bird is left

When police are catching criminals
There're always harsh sirens
If it is for ambulances or fire engines
It is easy to understand
But for police cars
Isn't this a rash act to alert the enemy?
Is it to show authority
Or to
Boost their courage

The half-removed community
Leaves only the broken walls and ruins
Wind drifts from one house to another
From time to time
Blows something to fly in the air

Straws and embraces are after all
Unreliable
I need nails
As many nails as possible
To fix me on the wall
Using the pain
To support me
To keep me from slipping
And becoming a mess
Certainly I know
Even if the last nail is pricked
Into my heart
I can't be
Jesus who's worshiped by everyone

Today's mood is a bit complicated
A patient with polio came to see the doctor
His right thumb was stretched
The other four fingers were bent
Kept the posture
Of give me a "Like"

You'll never see
My poems again
When saying this
The sun hasn't set yet
When finish saying
It sets

When I was young
I was inspiring and heroic
Drinking in a big bowl, eating meat in big mouthfuls
Using a knife to chop things that don't look good to me
Now I'm old
Edges and corners are all hidden
Using the knife to cut myself

After I die
If you miss me
Just give me a call
At first
The number you dialed is switched off
After that
The number you dialed is out of service due to arrears
Lastly
The number you dialed does not exist
Like everything
Had never happened

Notes

1   "Free Life Pond (放生池)" is an annex pond of the Han Chinese Buddhist temples. It embodies Buddhist thoughts of compassion and understanding of all living beings.

2   There is a Chinese idiom that says "corpses are wrapped in horse leather (马革裹尸)," often used to describe soldiers who died on the battlefield.

3   "Green train (绿皮火车)" is a nickname for the old-style trains; they are usually the slowest type, having as many stops as possible, usually having a green appearance.

4   "Kwan-yin Bodhisattva (观音菩萨)" is the Buddhist bodhisattva associated with compassion. In the East Asian world, Kwan-yin is the equivalent term for Avalokitesvara Bodhisattva.

5   "Li Sao (离骚)" is a Chinese poem from the anthology Chuci, can also be sung, dating from the Warring States period of ancient China, generally attributed to Qu Yuan (屈原).

6   "Red or white happy events (红白喜事)" is a Chinese idiom: "red" refers to marriage and birthday and "white" refers to a funeral. Since aging, sickness and death are all natural phenomena, death can also

be regarded as a natural end to a person, and it is a kind of relief; some Chinese also see a funeral as a happy event.

About the Author:

Zhou Li (周立) is a professional doctor, sometimes writes poems, and has published three books, having burned them all. Zhou Li says, "They are my life. I can decide on their existence and destruction."

About the Translator:

Xi Nan (Nancy, 西楠) was born in China. She writes and translates, is an indie publisher, and is the author of different genres. Her latest hybrid texts: *Brandy* (published by Alien Buddha Press). Her Twitter: @XiNan_Nancy

www.ingramcontent.com/pod-product-compliance
Lightning Source LLC
Chambersburg PA
CBHW031119080526
44587CB00011B/1032